ANCIENT CHINA

RUSSELL ROBERTS

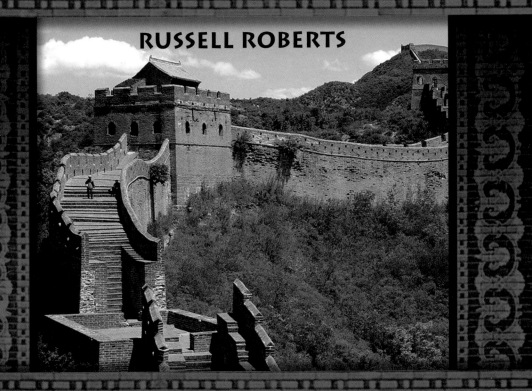

PUBLISHERS

P.O. Box 196
Hockessin, Delaware 19707
Visit us on the web: www.mitchelllane.com
Comments? email us: mitchelllane@mitchelllane.com

EXPLORE ANCIENT WORLDS

Ancient Assyria • Ancient Athens
The Aztecs • Ancient Babylon
The Byzantine Empire • The Celts of the British Isles
Ancient China • Ancient Egypt
Ancient India/Maurya Empire • Ancient Sparta

ABOUT THE AUTHOR: Russell Roberts has written and published nearly 40 books for adults and children, including C.C. Sabathia, Larry Fitzgerald, The Building of the Panama Canal, The Cyclopes, The Minotaur, The Battle of Hastings, and The Battle of Waterloo. He lives in Bordentown, New Jersey, with his family and a fat, fuzzy, and crafty calico cat named Rusti.

PUBLISHER'S NOTE: The facts on which the story in this book is based have been thoroughly researched. Documentation of such research can be found on page 45. While every possible effort has been made to ensure accuracy, the publisher will not assume liability for damages caused by inaccuracies in the data, and makes no warranty on the accuracy of the information contained herein.

Printing   1   2   3   4   5   6   7   8   9

Library of Congress
Cataloging-in-Publication Data
Roberts, Russell, 1953–
  Ancient China / by Russell Roberts.
    p. cm. — (Explore ancient worlds)
  Includes bibliographical references and index.
  ISBN 978-1-61228-277-0 (library bound)
  1. China—Civilization—To 221 B.C.—Juvenile literature. I. Title.
  DS741.65.R635 2012
  931—dc23
                                      2012008637

eBook ISBN: 9781612283524

PLB

CONTENTS

Chapter One
Incredible Rumor—Bizarre Story! 5
Sidebar: Qin Shi Huangdi and the Great Wall 9

Chapter Two
House, Home, and Clothing 11
Sidebar: The Discovery of Silk 15

Chapter Three
Men, Women and Food 17
Sidebar: Foot Binding 23

Chapter Four
Daily Life 25
Sidebar: Confucius 31

Chapter Five
The Truth Revealed 33
Sidebar: The Han Dynasty 37

Ancient Recipe: Chinese Corn Soup 38

Ancient Craft: Feng Shui 40

Timeline 42

Chapter Notes 44

Works Consulted 45
On the Internet 45

Further Reading 46

Glossary 47

Index 48

Emperor Qin Shi Huangdi

CHAPTER 1

Incredible Rumor— Bizarre Story!

It is late October, 210 BCE, and an incredible rumor is sweeping through many of the small farms in northern China, just outside the capital city of Xianyang. The rumor is that the mighty Chinese Emperor Qin Shi Huangdi is dead.

A group of farmers have gathered to discuss the news. Most of them say the same thing: Impossible!

Shi Huangdi's accomplishments have been momentous during his 11-year reign (221-210). He conquered and united China's various warring kingdoms into a single country. He developed a countrywide system of tree-lined roads 50 paces wide. To assure that all wheeled vehicles moved along the same ruts on these roads and not create a patchwork of indentations, he standardized the axle width of all vehicles. He ordered that the sections of walls built helter-skelter in the northern part of the country to keep out invaders be connected, creating a Great Wall 3,000 miles long.

The list goes on. He devised a national currency. He mandated a single standard writing style for the entire country, thereby creating a foundation for all future Chinese writing. He divided the country into 36 administrative units controlled by his officials, sweeping away centuries of feudal warlord control. He made 12 gigantic bronze bells from the weapons that he had confiscated. He went into the mountains and inscribed his achievements on them—a tribute he felt would last forever.

Indeed, Qin Shi Huangdi's impact on his land had been so great that his Qin (pronounced "chin") Dynasty had given the country the name by which it would be known throughout history: China. No wonder that in future centuries, many people would credit him with being the founder of modern China.

Yet Shi Huangdi also had a cruel streak that made people quake with fear. He buried over 400 scholars alive, burned books to wipe out any recorded history before he became emperor, instituted a harsh system of laws and punishments under a philosophy called Legalism, levied onerous taxes directly on the peasant farmers, and ruthlessly slaughtered whoever got in his way, often by barbarous methods such as tearing them apart by the limbs.

Sima Qian, described by some people as "the father of Chinese history," described Qin Shi Huangdi thusly: "A man with a prominent nose, large eyes, a chest like a bird of prey and the voice of a jackal; a man of little kindness, with a heart of a tiger, of that of a wolf."[1]

He had been born in 259 BCE with the name Ying Zheng. When he came to power he had declared himself Qin Shi Huangdi, which means "The First Emperor." He intended his reign to last for a thousand years or more, and sought a legendary immortality potion so that he, himself, could rule for much if not all of those thousand years.

How could such a man be dead, numerous farmers scoffed.

Yet the lord who owned these farms and had brought the news from Xianyang offered as proof a bizarre story he had been told by an official who had been part of the emperor's entourage and returned early.

The official explained that Qin Shi Huangdi had been away from Xianyang, on a tour of eastern China. This was not unusual, because the First Emperor liked to travel about China and did so frequently.[2] They had been about two months away from Xianyang when the emperor died. Li Si, the prime minister who had been traveling with the emperor, knew that Shi Huangdi's death was almost certain to cause unrest and turmoil.

By the time they got back to the capital, put a new leader in place, and re-established order, the empire itself could be shattered beyond repair if news of the death got out.

So Li Si decided to conceal the death. As the royal entourage began the journey back to the capital, only Li Si and a few others knew that Qin Shi Huangdi's carriage contained his lifeless body. That handful of men pretended to constantly talk to the emperor, and even changed his clothes daily.

Because the weather was warm, after several days the emperor's body began to decompose—and smell. To mask the foul stench coming from the carriage, Li Si ordered that all official carriages should carry a large supply of dried and rotting fish to camouflage Qin Shi Huangdi's own

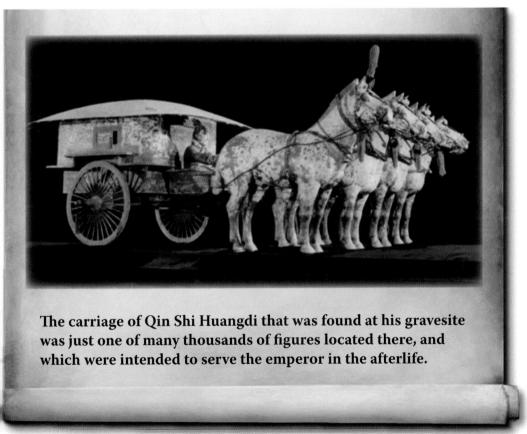

The carriage of Qin Shi Huangdi that was found at his gravesite was just one of many thousands of figures located there, and which were intended to serve the emperor in the afterlife.

**QIN DYNASTY
221–207 BCE**

GREAT WALL

Yellow R.

Xianyang

Wei R.

Yellow R.

QIN

Yangtse R.

CHINA

West R.

odor. The royal retinue was able to continue on its way with no one the wiser—just considerably smellier.

The farmers stared at each other. Their lord's story was bizarre—perhaps too bizarre to be made up. So was it possibly true? Was Qin Shi Huangdi really dead?

Qin Shi Huangdi and the Great Wall

In 215 BCE, at the command of Qin Shi Huangdi, Chinese general Meng Tian took an army of several hundred thousand men into northern China. He drove out two rebel tribes, the Rong and the Di, and then constructed a giant wall that, when finished, was approximately 3,000 miles long. Watchtowers with openings through which to shoot arrows at invaders were placed about several hundred yards apart.

The Great Wall

Actually, Tian did not build an entire wall that long. Rather, he connected sections of existing fortifications, building new walls where necessary. The walls were likely made of tamped earth. The modern Great Wall, made of masonry and one of China's most popular tourist destinations, is built on the foundations of this original wall.

It is commonly believed that Shi Huangdi had the wall built to keep invaders from the north out of China. The reason for the construction may have come when an oracle foretold that the emperor would be destroyed by a "Hu." Shi Huangdi took "Hu" to mean the nomadic tribes that roamed to the north of his kingdom.

According to most estimates, hundreds of thousands of people died constructing the wall. An ode from that time explains the average Chinese parent's despair at raising their children, only to have them die in the building of the wall: "If you have a son, don't raise him. If you have a girl, feed her dried meat. Can't you see, the Long Wall is propped up on skeletons."[3]

Peasant houses in ancient China were very small and made of whatever material they could find, since no one had money to buy more expensive materials. Often many generations lived together in just one room.

CHAPTER 2

House, Home, and Clothing

Homes in ancient China were essentially constructed in the same way for everyone, whether they were rich or poor. The difference between the two was in the size.

A peasant's house usually consisted of just one room, no matter how large the family was. The house was often constructed of mud bricks, which people made by mixing straw and water with moist clay. The clay was formed into the shape of a brick, either with a mold or by hand. The bricks were then dried by the sun until they formed a solid mass. The good thing about mud bricks was that there was plenty of earth and it was free, so materials were always available. Unfortunately, the rain chipped away at mud bricks, slowly eroding them and forcing them to be replaced periodically.

The roof of the house was made of thatch. Thatch was made by tying small bundles of grass or straw together. These bundles were then tightly overlaid on top of each other. Eventually the bundles became loose, so the roof had to be re-thatched every few years or it would leak. Later on, people who could afford it used tiles for roofing.

Surrounding each house was a wall made of rammed earth. One or more buildings faced out onto an interior courtyard. The courtyard had a gate in the south wall, which was considered the holy direction.[1]

All important buildings and all ancestral temples faced to the south. When a lord or ruler received subjects or guests, he faced south. Because the sun rose in the east, it was considered more honorable than the west. Thus when a host sat down facing south, he put his most honored guests on his right, facing east.[2]

The homes of the wealthy were usually made of materials such as mud bricks, but they were much larger, containing multiple rooms and sometimes even a second story. These homes often had numerous courtyards.

A security feature of ancient Chinese houses was a short wall that visitors encountered as soon as they walked through the doorway in the high surrounding wall. This was called a screen wall, and it prevented those who lived in the house from being immediately seen by anyone who just walked in.[3]

A small charcoal stove provided heat. Houses in northern China used a system of ducts and platforms made of raised bricks to send heat from the kitchen stove to a chimney. In colder weather mattresses were placed on the platforms for sleeping, since the platforms were warm.

In addition to the size of their houses, it was easy to tell who was rich and who was poor in ancient China by looking at their clothing. The rich wore very nice clothing, often made of silk that could be dyed. The poor wore clothing made of a coarser material called hemp.

Peasants wore a garment called a shen-i. It consisted of a tunic (like a long T-shirt) and a pair of pants. The tunic and pants were sewn together so that the shen-i was essentially one garment, although it had two parts. The sleeves were wide so that there was plenty of room for the arms. In fact, the entire shen-i fit very loosely. Since the shen-i was very plain, sometimes people would try to make it stand out by adding unique personal touches, such as sashes, colorful ribbons, or embroidery.

The garment was light in color and texture, which was standard for peasants to wear for doing everyday chores. Darker clothes were associated with ceremonial occasions.

The upper classes in ancient China wore much nicer and more elaborate clothing than peasants did, because their clothing did not have to stand up to hard work in the fields. The clothing of the wealthy was often made of expensive material and very colorful.

Peasants wore straw sandals. Even though they were basic, however, men were proud of these sandals, for they felt wearing them distinguished them from barefooted barbarians.[4] People from the upper classes wore fine cloth slippers that were often made of heavy damask or brocade.

Wealthy men and women dressed in trousers and long robes that were tied with a sash. These robes had elaborate patterns on them. The wearer's rank and status were indicated by the colors and shapes on the robes.

Silk clothing was not just a privilege—its use was a luxury that was tightly controlled by law. Only certain classes of people—for example, members of the emperor's court—could wear silk. If a person of a class that was forbidden to wear silk was caught wearing it, they could be severely punished.

Other rules pertaining to clothing involved colors. Yellow was a color reserved strictly for the emperor. During the Sui Dynasty, it was decreed that the poor could only wear blue or black-colored clothes.

Clothing colors were also used to display emotion. When someone died and a person was in mourning (a period of displaying grief), white

Clothing in ancient China was used to signify emotions. Red was a color used to show happiness, and so it was natural to use it for such occasions as weddings, such as in a wedding dress.

clothing was worn. On the other hand, people who were happy or joyful wore red clothing to signify these feelings.

By the third century BCE, clothing styles began to change, partly because of influences by northern nomad groups. Becoming popular then were underwear, leather pants and shoes, and leather belts with jeweled hooks.

An interesting item of clothing that some people wore were mirrors made from polished brass. It was believed that the mirrors provided protection from evil spirits. People wore them hanging down from the waist by a cord. Mirrors were also placed in graves to provide light for the dead.

The Discovery of Silk

Silk was discovered in ancient China. Several legends offer different versions of the way that the discovery happened. A popular story says that Lei Zu (her name is spelled several different ways), a consort of Emperor Huangdi, was drinking tea under some mulberry trees in the

A silkworm and its cocoon

Imperial Gardens. She accidentally dropped a silkworm cocoon into a cup of hot water. The cocoon unraveled into a long, delicate thread. Lei Zu found that these threads could be twisted together to form one strong yet very soft thread that could then be used to make a beautiful ceremonial robe for the emperor. Lei Zu also supposedly discovered how to raise silkworms, and invented the silk reel and the silk loom.

Another story is that a family had a flying horse. One day the father did not come home. His daughter was worried and said she'd marry the flying horse if he found her father. The horse did find him, but the father killed the animal rather than let his daughter marry him. However, the horse's skin picked up the girl and transported her to a tree. The moment the girl touched the tree, she turned into a silkworm and began producing silk.

A third story is that some Chinese women picked up silkworm cocoons from the ground, not knowing what they were. At first they tried to eat the cocoons, but couldn't. Angered, they beat the cocoons with sticks. Eventually the beating revealed the threads.

Silk was one of the most important discoveries made by the ancient Chinese. Although exactly how it was discovered is a mystery, its softness soon made it incredibly popular, and many Chinese were employed in making silk garments.

Men, Women, and Food

It is an unfortunate fact that females were not valued as much as males in Chinese society. Females were not thought of as highly because they could not carry forth the family name. Some fathers killed their daughters at birth. Others divorced their wives when they kept giving birth to daughters instead of sons. Some poor families even sold their daughters to rich people to be used as servants.

Virtually from birth, a Chinese female was taught to be subservient to males. Families would even sometimes let female babies in their cradles lie on the floor while male babies were placed higher to symbolize the inferiority of the female.

The best-known indication regarding the lower status of Chinese females was the infamous practice of foot-binding. It began around the beginning of the Tang Dynasty (618-907 CE), and lasted until the early 20th century.

Males were also preferred in a family from the basic standpoint of economics. Once a girl married, she became part of her husband's family, and so was lost to her own family. Thus all of the expense the family had incurred raising the girl was lost with no benefit.

Females were associated with the Yin, the doctrines of darkness and evil. Males, on the other hand, were considered as bringing good fortune—

Confucius was a teacher and philosopher who lived in ancient China. His wisdom is still relevant and followed today by people who quote him and try to live their lives by his principles. This giant sculpture of him is part of a new exhibition at the Rockbund Art Museum in Shanghai.

the Yang. So, to protect them from evil spirits, boys were sometimes given female names.[1]

This view of males and females was reinforced by Confucius, one of the most famous Chinese thinkers and philosophers, and developer of a school of thought that many people followed. The world that Confucius envisioned was one controlled by men.

Once early childhood had passed, girls and boys did not play together anymore. While boys, when possible, went to school to prepare themselves for civil service examinations—for which girls were ineligible—females were taught how to manage a household and how to take care of their husbands, children, and mothers-in-law. However, sometimes even this type of education was ignored, and a girl who was married had to learn "on the job" after she was married, under the harsh scrutiny of her mother-in-law.

Things did not get any easier for a woman after she was married. If she had any property at all, it came under her husband's control. A female not only had to have children and raise them, she also had to take care of the house and help in the fields. She could be divorced by her husband for numerous reasons, such as not giving birth to a son, but a woman could not divorce her husband. While a man could have only one wife according to law, he could take as many concubines, or lovers, as he could afford.[2] A woman who had a son was given much respect and honor, while a woman who did not was shunned.

Often peasants lived in their one-room houses with their entire family. The wealthy also had their entire family living in their house. Although the home was much bigger, as many as 100 people could be living together.

The father was the undisputed leader of the family, and his word was accepted without question, particularly by his children. Whether or not a boy went to school was strictly up to his father, who determined if the boy could be spared from working in the fields. Most boys worked in the fields. Girls were rarely sent to school.

Honoring one's ancestors was very important. The Chinese believed that upon a man's death, his spirit would continue to exert influence upon his earthly descendants.

A father realized that one day, he too would be an ancestor. So it was vital to him to make his children revere him when he was alive so that they would continue to do so after his death. As the father aged, he achieved an exalted status within the household. It was not uncommon for even wealthy lords to sew and patch their father's robe with their own hands.

It was customary for both men and women to wear their hair long. It was felt that hair came from one's parents, and that it was disrespectful to cut it. Short hair was usually only found on prisoners, who were given it as a punishment. Monks were an exception to this custom, as they sometimes shaved their hair to indicate that they didn't care about worldly things such as appearance or long hair.

Men tied their hair in a topknot, and used elaborate hairpins to hold the topknot in place. By the time of the Tang Dynasty, a top-knot wrapping or a gauze cap stiffened with lacquer became the fashion.

Women braided their hair and coiled it up onto their heads. They used hairpins for decoration. A female was not allowed to curl her hair with hairpins until she was married.

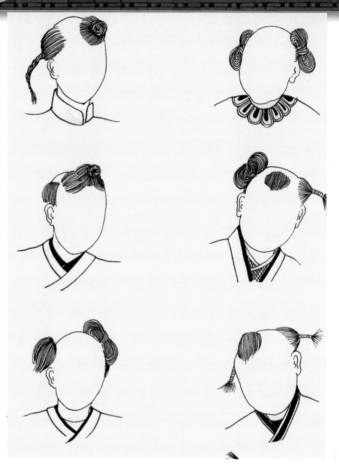

Hair styles for children

The Chinese ate two meals, one at mid-morning and the other in the evening. Children took food to their parents before eating themselves, and bowed to the elders in the family.

In the northern part of China, millet was a dietary staple. Other popular foods were beans, turnips, and melons. These foods might be flavored with onions, ginger, or noodles, bread, or basil. A typical meal might consist of wheat noodles, bread and bean curd. The food was served in small bowls. The entire family sat around a sunken pit in the middle of the house, which was the location of a fire used for both heating and cooking.

People who lived in the south of China ate rice, for it grew easily there in the area's marshy wetlands. They supplemented that basic staple with taro root.

The wealthy might add some fish, eggs, chicken and meat to their meals. They also tended to steam or stir-fry their food.

Initially people drank the fermented products of the cereal grains they had grown, such as millet and rice. Other drinks included coconut milk and grape wine.

Tea, which people often associate with China, does not appear in Chinese documentation until the second half of the third century CE,

Rice grew easily in southern China because of the area's wet weather and the fact that much of the land was marshy. Not only did they eat it, but peasants also made rice into wine and drank it as well.

Tea is so common today, it's funny to think that at one time it was only known in China. Once it was discovered, however, it quickly spread, first throughout China and then to other parts of the world.

although it almost certainly was known and drunk before that time. Tea drinking was initially confined to southern China, but it gradually spread northward. By the 700s rich and poor alike were drinking tea. Tea was not grown on large plantations. Instead, each household grew their own plants for their own individual use.[10]

Foot Binding

When a Chinese girl was between the ages of four and eight, her parents would bind her feet. Her feet were bandaged with strips of white cloth in such a manner that the four toes of each foot—minus the big toe—were bent in under the sole of the foot. This forced her to walk on the joints of the bent toes, which was extremely painful.

Typical shoes for foot-bound women

The girl's foot was also shortened by wrapping bandages tightly around it in such a way that the ball of the foot was forced almost back to the heel. This caused the arch of the foot to bend upwards like an archer's drawn bow.

The bandages were continually pulled tighter to assure that no growth could occur. Besides the obvious pain that the action caused by itself, girls had to walk a certain amount each day so their feet would not get diseased. Thus they were putting the full weight of their body on their tightly bound feet, resulting in even more pain. According to a Chinese saying, "For every pair of bound feet there is a big tub full of tears."[4]

This process continued for several years. The end result was a pair of small, pointed feet between three and six inches long. Tiny feet were considered very pretty in China. Parents of all social classes did foot binding because they were afraid their daughters would never marry if they had regular-sized feet. The practice continued into the 20th century, when it was finally banned.

The Chinese invented the iron plow, which was a vast improvement over the other types, such as wood, that were then in existence. The strength and durability of the iron plow enabled Chinese farmers to get more work done in a shorter time.

CHAPTER 4

Daily Life

The life of peasant farmers was hard. Some of them might own the small plot of land they farmed, but many did not and instead worked for a rich man who owned the land. In return for letting the farmer use the land, the rich man received half of the harvest. The farmer also had to send some of his harvest to the government. He and his family had to survive on what was left.

To help feed his family, a peasant had to catch small animals and fish. However, even here he couldn't always win. During certain periods of the Han Dynasty (206 BCE–220 CE), fish were taxed.

Farmers used numerous methods to wring every ounce of growing power out of the soil. Ashes and dung were used as fertilizer. A crop rotation system was instituted so that the same crops were not planted in the same place every year, helping the soil retain specific nutrients.

They also planted seeds in rows to increase crop yields. Chinese farmers were the first ever to plant this way, rather than just scattering seeds randomly.[1]

Another factor was the iron plow, which was invented in China. When other countries were using less durable designs made of wood or rope, the Chinese were using iron to prepare the ground for seeding.[2] In the north oxen pulled the plows, while water buffalo were used in the south.

The wheelbarrow is yet another invention of the Chinese, which they were using centuries before Europeans. The wheelbarrow was especially useful for transporting heavy loads on the narrow paths between fields that the Chinese farmer had to navigate.

In the north of China wheat, millet and barley were common crops. In the wetter south, rice was usually grown.

The lack of adequate rainfall was a constant problem in northern China. In other areas the problem was too much water, a result of frequent flooding. Farmers tried to solve these problems by developing and becoming masters of irrigation systems that brought water from nearby rivers into the fields and controlled its flow. One type, for example, involved people operating foot pedals. These pedals powered a pulley system that sent a series of buckets down into a river. These buckets scooped up water and then traveled up the pulleys to the end, where the water was dumped out into a series of canals that flowed to the various fields.

Human-powered pumps are still found in Asia

The ancient Chinese quickly became masters of irrigation systems – how to build them, how to make them operate, and how to make them last. The Dujiangyan Irrigation System, built long ago and still operational, is proof of this.

They also built large-scale irrigation systems, both to control the amount of water at any one time as well as to assure adequate water in areas of less-frequent rain. In fact, the Dujiangyan Irrigation System, built in 256 BCE, still survives and functions today. It is the oldest operational irrigation system in the world that diverts water without the use of a dam.

Farming was extremely important in ancient China. Every spring, once the weather warmed, the Chinese king went to a field near his palace and with his own hands plowed a few rows. Then his ministers took turns each plowing a few more rows. This field was called the Field of God. Crops raised on this field could be used only for sacrifices.[3]

Yet despite the importance that Chinese culture and society placed on farming, peasants could be yanked away from their farms at a moment's notice to serve as foot soldiers in the army of whatever ruler was in power at the moment. Once that occurred, a farmer often had little hope of returning to his former life. If he was not killed in battle, then he might well be captured and killed, or else sold into slavery. A Chinese folk song described the plight of the farmer-turned-soldier: "Long ago, when we started, the willows spread their shade. Now that we turn back the snowflakes fly. The march before us is long, we are thirsty and hungry, our hearts are stricken with sorrow but no one listens to our plaint."[4]

Because farming was so hard and took so much time and effort, peasants had little time left over for leisure activities. However, they did enjoy a few things.

Hunting was a sport that all classes of Chinese society, from peasant to emperor, enjoyed. There was a game that resembled modern football in some respects, and was considered as good practice for the military. Board and table games were also played. Other leisure pursuits included bull and cock-fighting, archery, and races.

The higher one's station, the more time was available to engage in amusements. Without the need to work, wealthy Chinese men and women had much more free time on their hands. Parlor games, music, and dancing were some of the activities enjoyed by the nobility. During the Tang Dynasty polo became popular. Playing cards and dominoes, invented by the Chinese, were also popular pastimes.

The ancient Chinese invented numerous things that had a significant impact on daily life. One is paper, which is thought to have been invented around the first century CE and for which the Chinese found many uses. Prior to this, books were written on slips of bamboo or wood. As can be imagined, books made in this way were heavy and bulky. Silk was even tried for book-printing, but the expense of the material made this option unrealistic.

According to legend, a man named Ts'ai Lun was the inventor of paper. He mixed the inner bark of a mulberry tree with water and bamboo fibers. He took the mixture and pounded it with a wooden tool until it was flat and thin. He then placed the entire mixture on a piece of coarse cloth. The water drained through the cloth and left a paste on top. Once

The invention of block printing was a tremendous leap forward in learning and education. Books could be printed faster and in greater quantity, so more people could read them.

it dried, Ts'ai Lun discovered that he had devised a light, yet tough, writing surface.

The Chinese also invented woodblock printing. The first woodblock book with a definite date was produced around 868 CE, though the actual invention was probably a few centuries earlier. In about 1040, the Chinese invented movable type. Johannes Gutenberg did not invent the printing press using movable type in Europe until the mid-1400s.

The magnetic compass was yet another Chinese invention. It enabled them determine the correct direction. At first they used the compass to help lay out houses so that they faced the correct direction to be in harmony with Nature. Later the compass found other uses, such as by

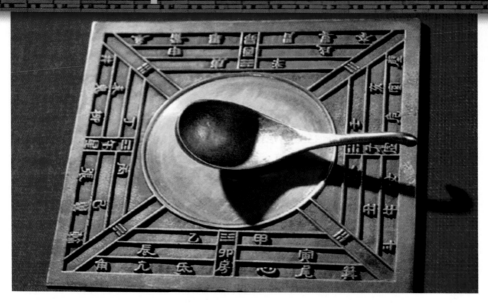

Another important invention by the ancient Chinese was the compass. It helped travelers, ship captains, and others to determine the proper direction, taking the guesswork out of the process.

map makers and for the navigation of ships. The compass consisted of a magnetic needle floating in water, known as a "wet" compass.

Gunpowder was invented in 850 CE during the Tang Dynasty. A Chinese alchemist, searching for an immortality potion, mixed together saltpeter, sulfur and charcoal. The mixture exploded when it was exposed to an open flame.

These four inventions—printing, paper, gunpowder, and the compass—all had a significant impact on the daily life of the Chinese people. Sometimes these four inventions are called the Four Great Inventions of ancient China.

Other important inventions of the ancient Chinese were the rudder for steering large ships, the umbrella (for protection from the sun as well as the rain), hot air balloons, matches, and the seismograph (a machine to measure earthquakes).

Confucius

Silk, paper and gunpowder had a great effect on humanity. So did the teachings of a Chinese thinker and philosopher named Confucius, born in 551 BCE.

Confucius' tomb

He studied music, playing the lute (a musical instrument), and ritual, which is the proper way to do certain things. He gathered a group of followers to whom he taught his philosophies. At the age of 50 he briefly held a job serving Duke Ding of the Chinese state of Lu. However, he lost this job and was forced into exile. After wandering about China for some time he returned to Lu in 484 BCE. He remained there until his death in 479 BCE, teaching his philosophies of life.

These teachings are presented in a series of books called the Analects. He felt that people were basically good, and that government should act kindly and be responsible. This view was in direct conflict with the later philosophy of Qin Shi Huangdi, which held that people were bad and needed to be kept in line by harsh laws and strict punishment.

Confucius also preached respect for the family, especially the older members. He encouraged creativity, and felt that arts such as painting and music were important to a happy life. Above all, he urged people to always try to expand their knowledge through education.

According to Confucius, people were responsible for their own actions, and for their treatment of others. People can determine how they are remembered and what they can accomplish in life.

The tomb of Qin Shi Huangdi was not discovered for thousands of years, and then only by accident. It was uncovered by farmers trying to place water pipes. Its discovery is now one of the most famous and significant of all time.

CHAPTER
5

The Truth
Revealed

The farmers continue to talk excitedly about whether or not the First Emperor, Qin Shi Huangdi, could actually be dead. Many still maintain that his death is impossible. One tells a story to illustrate that point.

His noble lord once told him that Qin Shi Huangdi had gone to seven sacred mountains and placed seven stelae (stone pillars) engraved with statements about him and his achievements on these mountains. The inscription on the last stelae said: "His virtuous power and favour is permanent and lasting."[1]

Now, says the farmer forcefully, how could such a man as that, who had proclaimed his permanency to the heavens in our sacred mountains, be dead? It is impossible! Qin Shi Huangdi will live forever!

However, just as voices are raised to a fever pitch, a traveler from Xianyang approaches on the nearby road. Within minutes he confirms the news to the excited farmers: The mighty Qin Shi Huangdi is indeed dead.

The traveler says that the emperor's entourage arrived in the capital city several days ago, bearing his body. Shi Huangdi was scared of death, says the traveler, who was a court official and knew the emperor. He never wanted to hear about death, or hear about funerals.[2] He searched incessantly for a drug that guaranteed immortality for anyone who took it.

At one point the emperor sent an alchemist named Xu Fu on a fleet of ships with thousands of young men and women—who were to be the payment for the drug—to search for an island of immortals, where this drug was supposed to be found. The fleet never returned. It has been claimed that the fleet reached Japan and colonized it.[3]

However, Xu Fu returned to China, and one day Qin Shi Huangdi encountered him. The alchemist convinced the First Emperor that he could have easily brought the drug back from the island if only it hadn't been for large sharks. So the emperor took his revenge by standing on the shoreline and shooting arrows at passing sharks.[4]

The official speculated that the First Emperor was anxious to gain immortality because he had been the target of several assassination attempts. The one that almost succeeded, he said, was by a man named Jing Ke. Ke, along with an accomplice, was supposed to present a map

Qin Shi Huangdi was terrified of dying, so he was always alert to any possibility of being attacked and murdered. One way he tried to prevent attacks was by having a large group of guards around him.

and other gifts to the emperor. Ke rolled up the map and put a poisoned dagger inside. However, as the two approached Shi Huangdi in his palace to give him the gift, the accomplice lost his nerve and stopped, leaving Ke to face the emperor alone. Ke unrolled his map, pulled out the dagger, grabbed the emperor by the sleeve of his robe and struck at him.

Shi Huangdi was too fast. He darted back as Ke lunged at him, tearing off the sleeve of his robe. Ke threw the empty sleeve to the floor and chased after the emperor, who had run behind a pillar. Because of his fear of death, Shi Huangdi had forbidden anybody in the palace except himself to have weapons. So the other court officials watched in helpless shock as Ke chased after their emperor. Fortunately, a quick-thinking doctor named Xia Wuju who was present sprang forward and hit Jing Ke with his medicine bag, which distracted him and gave the First Emperor time to draw his weapon.

Jing Ke charged Shi Huangdi again, but this time the emperor managed to wound him in the leg. Ke threw the poisoned dagger at the emperor but missed. Realizing he had failed, Jing Ke laughed and leaned against a pillar. By now the crowd had recovered from its shock and fell upon Jing Ke, killing him.

Now Qin Shi Huangdi was dead, killed not by an assassin but by natural causes. The official feared chaos and anarchy with the emperor dead. He could not have been more right.

With Qin Shi Huangdi dead, the reign of the Qin Dynasty, which was intended to last for centuries, quickly fell apart. The scheming of Chinese officials was to blame. Shi Huangdi had intended his oldest son Fusu to succeed him and before he died he sent him a message to that effect. However, another son named Huhai and his tutor, Zhao Gao, intercepted the message and replaced it with another demanding that Fusu kill himself because he had spoken badly about his father's time as emperor. Fusu complied, and Huhai became emperor, with Zhao Gao as his adviser. However, Huhai was a harsh and terrible ruler, demanding even more taxes from the peasants. Within a year revolts had toppled him.

The Terra Cotta Warriors in the tomb of Qin Shi Huangdi consist of thousands of figures of different types and in different poses. They have become world famous, and China has sent some of them on traveling exhibitions to countries around the world.

Ironically, according to legend the rebels armed themselves by breaking into Qin Shi Huangdi's tomb and taking weapons out of the hands of an army of thousands of statues of warriors that Qin Shi Huangdi had made to protect and serve him in the afterlife—the famous Terra Cotta Warriors.

The Terra Cotta Warriors are a group of approximately 8,000 life-sized terra cotta statues of soldiers, chariots, horses, jugglers, musicians, and others. They were discovered accidentally in 1974 by a group of farmers who were digging a well about one mile from the tomb of Qin Shi Huangdi.

The figures are in three massive underground cave-like rooms with wooden ceilings. Some of the figures' weapons—swords, spears, crossbows—are missing, which supports the story that the rebels took these weapons and used them themselves. There is also evidence of fire damage in spots in the pits, further indicating that something happened in there.

Work on this massive terra cotta army began soon after Qin Shi Huangdi took over the throne in 246 BCE. Thus the First Emperor spent much of his life having figures built that he hoped would protect and serve him in the afterlife. If these figures did indeed help bring about the fall of his dynasty, then it was this life, not the afterlife, that Qin Shi Huangdi should have been concerned about.

The Han Dynasty

The Han Dynasty followed the Qin Dynasty. It lasted from 206 BCE to 220 CE. During this time the Chinese people enjoyed economic success. They also tried to repair some of the damage done during the rule of Qin Shi Huangdi.

Han character

During the Han Dynasty, the famous Silk Road was established. The Silk Road was not actually one road, but rather a series of trading routes between China and Rome, India, and other countries. The Chinese traded silk—which the Romans and others greatly desired—for gold, silver, and other things. They also used it for many other trade goods, such as ivory and spices. The booming trade along the Silk Road helped China become prosperous.

During the Han Dynasty, an effort was made to replace the knowledge and information that had been destroyed when Qin Shi Huangdi ordered the burning of so many books. One special target was to bring back the wisdom of Confucius that had been lost. Because Confucius had placed so much importance on education, a system of public schools was established—although only for males.

The Han Dynasty was a time of artistic rebirth in China. Works of literature and music were created, and beautiful murals were painted on walls. Craftsmen created jewelry out of jade and gold.

Medicine and industry also progressed during the Han Dynasty. Acupuncture was invented, as was paper. Newer and sturdier tools made of iron, such as plows, were devised. These tools led to increases in agricultural production, which meant more food for everyone.

Ancient Recipe: Chinese Corn Soup

INGREDIENTS

- 1 egg, beaten
- Cornstarch (1 tablespoon)
- Water (2 tablespoons)
- 1 can (15 ounces) of cream-style corn
- 1 can (14.5 ounces) of low-sodium chicken broth

DIRECTIONS

1. Put creamed corn and chicken broth into a saucepan.
2. Boil the ingredients over medium-high heat.
3. Put cornstarch and water into a small bowl.
4. Pour this mixture into the corn/broth in the saucepan.
5. Cook the entire mixture until it thickens – about two minutes.
6. Stir the soup, adding the beaten egg while you do so.
7. It's ready to eat.

Ancient Craft: Feng Shui

Feng shui, which means "wind and water," is the ancient Chinese art of determining how energy, or qi (pronounced "chee") flows through a room or house. Feng shui promotes prosperity, good health, and general well-being.

You can make a bamboo arrangement to help bring a positive qi to any room. The materials you'll need are bamboo stalks, gold/silver foundation stones, container, a red ribbon, and water.

The five elements of feng shui are earth (represented by the stones), water (the water you use in your arrangement), wood (the bamboo stalks), fire (red ribbon), and metal (the color gold or silver). You can also use little figurines or ornaments of metal or metallic covering.

The type of energy you are trying to achieve depends upon the number of bamboo stalks in the arrangement. The number of bamboo stalks means: 1-simplicity, 2-double luck, 3-prosperity/fertility, 4-academic achievement, 5-happiness, 6-easy money, 7-good luck in relationships, 8-good luck/fertility, 9-good health, 10-fulfillment in life.

DIRECTIONS

1. Place the number of bamboo stalks you wish to use into the empty container.
2. Put the foundation stones in until the bamboo stalks are stable.
3. Add water. The bamboo roots must be covered.
4. Add figurine/ornament if desired.
5. Tie the red ribbon around the container.

Congratulations! You've just helped bring a positive qi to a room!

BCE

4000-2205   The Chinese farm around the Yellow River Valley, growing crops such as millet, rice and wheat. Pigs, cows, chickens and other livestock are domesticated.

2205-1766   The Chinese discover how to make tools and weapons from bronze.

City-states are formed in China and used for social and political organization.

The Hsia (or Xia) Dynasty is formed when a man named Yu drains flood waters and becomes the first king.

1766-1050   The Shang Dynasty overthrows the Hsia Dynasty.

Society begins to divide into upper and lower classes.

A writing system emerges.

Ancestor worship develops.

Jade carvings, stone carvings, bronze work, and other art forms flourish.

Use of the chariot becomes common.

Water buffalo and various types of birds are domesticated.

1050-256   The Chou (or Zhou) Dynasty overthrows the Shang Dynasty. The Chou Dynasty develops the notion of the Mandate from Heaven, meaning that they rule with the approval of the Supreme Deity. This notion becomes a staple of Chinese rule for many centuries.

Lao-Zu is born about 560 BCE; he develops philosophy of Taoism.

Confucius born around 551 BCE; he develops philosophy of Confucianism.

Iron is discovered and used to improve agriculture methods. This leads to a food surplus and population growth.

In 481 BCE, the various city-states begin warring with each other.

Confucius dies around 479 BCE.

Folding umbrella developed around 300 BCE.

256-206 Chou Dynasty ends and one city-state—Qin—eventually becomes powerful enough to rule all of China.

In 221 BCE, Qin Shi Huangdi, the first emperor of China, completes reunification of the city-states. China is now one country. Qin Shi Huangdi standardizes weights and measurements, the money system, and even writing.

The first Great Wall of China is constructed.

A country-wide network of roads and canals is built.

Philosophy of Legalism is developed.

Qin Shi Huangdi dies in 210 BCE, leading to a scramble for power. Ultimately the dynasty that he had hoped would rule for centuries crumbles after just four years.

206–220 CE The Han Dynasty is established in 206 BCE and China enjoys a long period of peace and prosperity.

A new religion—Buddhism–is introduced into China

Paper is created around 105 CE.

Tea developed around 200 CE.

Chapter One: Incredible Rumor—Bizarre Story
1. Julia Lovell, *The Great Wall* (New York: Grove Press, 2006), p. 47.
2. Kenneth Scott Latourette, *The Chinese* (New York: The Macmillan Company, 1967), p. 69.
3. Lovell, *The Great Wall,* p. 60.

Chapter Two: House, Home, and Clothing
1. Edward H. Schafer, *Ancient China* (New York: Time-Life Books, 1967), p. 39.
2. Elizabeth Seeger, *The Pageant of Chinese History* (New York: David McKay Company, Inc., 1972), p. 53.
3. KIDIPEDE: Ancient Chinese Houses
http://www.historyforkids.org/learn/china/architecture/chinesehouses.htm
4. Schafer, *Ancient China,* p. 39.

Chapter Three: Men, Women and Food
1. Kenneth Scott Latourette, *The Chinese* (New York: The Macmillan Company, 1967), p. 574.
2. Ibid, p. 570.
3. L. Carrington Goodrich, *A Short History of the Chinese People* (New York: Harper & Brothers, 1959), p. 80.
4. Elizabeth Seeger, *The Pageant of Chinese History* (New York: David McKay Company, Inc., 1972), p. 203.

Chapter Four: Daily Life
1. Ancient Chinese Farming Techniques
http://www.ehow.com/list_6885466_ancient-chinese-farming-techniques.html
2. Ibid.
3. Elizabeth Seeger, *The Pageant of Chinese History* (New York: David McKay Company, Inc., 1972), p. 47.
4. Edward H. Schafer, *Ancient China* (New York: Time-Life Books, 1967), p. 27.

Chapter Five: The Truth Revealed
1. John Man, *The Terra Cotta Army* (Cambridge, Massachusetts: Da Capo Press, 2008), p. 93.
2. Kenneth Scott Latourette, *The Chinese* (New York: The Macmillan Company, 1967), p. 73.
3. Ibid.
4. Julia Lovell, *The Great Wall* (New York: Grove Press, 2006), p. 61.

Fairbank, John King. *China: A New History.* Cambridge, Massachusetts: The Belknap Press of Harvard University Press, 1992.

Goodrich, L. Carrington. *A Short History of the Chinese People.* New York: Harper & Brothers Publishers, 1959.

Latourette, Kenneth Scott. *The Chinese.* New York: The Macmillan Company, 1967.

Lovell, Julia. *The Great Wall.* New York: Grove Press, 2006.

Man, John. *The Terra Cotta Army.* Cambridge, Massachusetts: Da Capo Press, 2008.

Paludan, Ann. *Chronicle of the Chinese Emperors.* London, England: Thames and Hudson Ltd., 1998.

Schafer, Edward H. *Ancient China.* New York: Time-Life Books, 1967.

Seeger, Elizabeth. *The Pageant of Chinese History.* New York: David McKay Company, Inc., 1972.

The Cambridge Encyclopedia of China. Brian Hook, editor. Cambridge, Massachusetts: Cambridge University Press, 1991.

On the Internet

Ancient Chinese Farming Techniques
http://www.ehow.com/list_6885466_ancient-chinese-farming-tech niques.html

KIDIPEDE: Ancient Chinese Houses
http://www.historyforkids.org/learn/china/architecture/chinesehous es.htm

Feng Shui Cures
http://fengshui.about.com/od/fengshuicures/qt/luckybamboo.ht mhttp://fengshui.about.com/od/fengshuicures/qt/luckybamboo.htm

Books

Anderson, Dale. *Ancient China*. Chicago, Illinois: Raintree, 2005.

Dubois, Muriel L., *Ancient China: Beyond the Great Wall.* North Mankato, Minnesota: Capstone Press, 2011.

Fine, Jil, *Writing In Ancient China.* Boston, Massachusetts: Rigby, 2009.

Hessler, Peter. *Oracle Bones: A Journey Between China's Past and Present.* New York: HarperCollins, 2006.

Kramer, Lance. *Great Ancient China Projects.* White River Junction, Vermont: Nomad Press, 2008.

O'Connor, Jane. *Hidden Army: Clay Soldiers of Ancient China.* New York: Grosset & Dunlop, 2011.

Steele, Philip. *The Chinese Empire.* New York: Rosen Central, 2008.

On the Internet

Ancient China for Kids
http://china.mrdonn.org/

KIDIPEDE: Ancient China
http://www.historyforkids.org/learn/china/

KIDIPEDE: Ancient Chinese Houses
http://www.historyforkids.org/learn/china/architecture/chinesehouses.htm

Ancient China
http://www.crystalinks.com/china.html

Ancient China
http://www.historylink101.com/china_history.html

Glossary

alchemist (AL-kuh-mist) – person who tries to change common materials into previous metals such as gold.

barbarous (BAHR-buh-russ) – savage; cruel.

brocade (bro-KADE) – heavy fabric with an interwoven raised design or pattern.

camouflage (KAM-uh-flazh) – disguise or hide something.

consort (KON-sort) – spouse.

damask (DAM-uhsk) – a reversible fabric of linen, silk, cotton, or wool woven with patterns.

decompose (dee-cuhm-POZE) – to rot.

diverts (dih-VURTZ) – turns aside.

durable (DUHR-uh-bull) – resistant to wear.

dynasty (DIE-nuss-tee) – a ruling family or group.

entourage (AWN-too-razh) – a group of personal attendants.

envisioned (ehn-VIHZ-uhnd) – pictured mentally.

hemp (HEMP) – the tough fiber of the moraceous plant, used for making rope, coarse fabric, and other things.

mandated (MAN-day-tuhd) – issued an authoritative order or command.

masonry (MAY-suhn-ree)- stonework or brickwork.

momentous (mo-MEN-tuss) – serious.

nutrients (NEW-tree-ehntz) – something that nourishes.

ode (ODE) – a poem of heightened emotion.

onerous (AH-nuh-russ) – oppressive.

plaint (PLAYNT) – complaint.

retinue (REH-tih-noo) – those who serve an important person.

revere (ree-VEAR) – regard with great respect.

subservient (sub-SUHR-vee-uhnt) – acting in a subordinate manner.

tamped (TAMPT) – firmly packed a substance down.

Compass 30

Confucius 18, 31

Di 9

Dujiangyan Irrigation System
27

Field of God 27

foot binding 17, 23

Fu, Xu 34

Gao, Zhao 35

Gunpowder 30

Guttenberg, Johannes 29

Hair styles 19, 20

Han Dynasty 25, 37

Huangdi, Qin Shi 4-9, 33-37

Huhai 35

Iron Plow 24,25

irrigation systems 26

Ke, Jing 34, 35

Lun, Ts'ai 28

millet 20, 26

Qian, Sima 6, 36

Qin Dynasty 35

Rockbund Art Museum 18

Rong 9

Screen wall 12

Shen-i 1

Si, Li 7,8

Silk 13, 15, 16

Silk Road 37

Sui Dynasty 13

Tang Dynasty 17, 28, 30

Terra Cotta Warriors 36

Tian, Meng 9

thatch 11

Woodblock printing 2

Wuju, Xia 35

Xianyang 5-7, 33

Yang 18

Yin 17

Zheng, Ying 6

Zu, Lei 15